IN FOCUS...
FOOTBALL

DENNIS PERNU

Quarto is the authority on a wide range of topics.

Quarto educates, entertains and enriches the lives of our readers—enthusiasts and lovers of hands-on living.

www.quartoknows.com

This library edition published in 2019
by Quarto Library,
an imprint of The Quarto Group.
6 Orchard Road
Suite 100
Lake Forest, CA 92630
T: +1 949 380 7510
F: +1 949 380 7575
www.QuartoKnows.com

Distributed in the United States and Canada by Lerner Publisher Services
241 First Avenue North
Minneapolis, MN 55401 U.S.A.
www.lernerbooks.com

A CIP record for this book is available from the Library of Congress.

ISBN 978 0 7112 4796 3

Manufactured in Guangdong, China CC072019

9 8 7 6 5 4 3 2 1

MIX
Paper from responsible sources
FSC® C008047

CONTENTS

FOOTBALL HISTORY

Like baseball, football grew from other sports. American players added their own rules to other games. Over time, the sport became football as we know it today. At first football was very violent. In the early 1900s, some even felt it should be outlawed.

Football grew out of college sports. This drawing shows the Yale and Columbia university teams playing in 1901. The leather helmets provided little protection.

Chaotic College Games

In the 1800s, teams from American colleges played sports that used rules from rugby and soccer. The first of these games was played in 1869 between Rutgers and Princeton. Every college had different rules. In 1873, a small group of colleges created one set of rules to follow. These rules allowed 20 players per team to be on the field. Games could be brutal.

In football's early days players wore only shirts and perhaps thinly padded pants. This is the 1891 Rutgers team.

WOW!
In 1905 19 men were killed and more than 150 were injured playing football.

Game Changers

Walter Camp is considered "the father of American football." Camp played for Yale University. In 1880 he introduced the **hike**, or the "snap," to football. He also suggested that each team have 11 players on the field and proposed a system of downs. In 1905, US President Teddy Roosevelt called a summit of football advisors to help make football less dangerous. His own son had been badly injured playing for Harvard. The field was reduced to its current size and the forward pass was made legal.

Walter Camp is credited for suggesting many rule changes that today's football fans take for granted.

5

KICKOFF TIME

Some football games are played in huge stadiums before 100,000 fans. Others are played in small parks with just a few spectators. But from youth levels all the way to the National Football League (NFL), teams play on a field with the same measurements and follow the same general rules.

The Football Field

Football games take place on a field. The playing area is 100 yards (91.4 meters) long and there are two 10-yard-long (9.14-meter-long) end zones. Games begin with a **kickoff** and are split into four 15-minute quarters.

The field has a white line every yard (0.91 meters) and a number every 10 yards (9.14 meters).

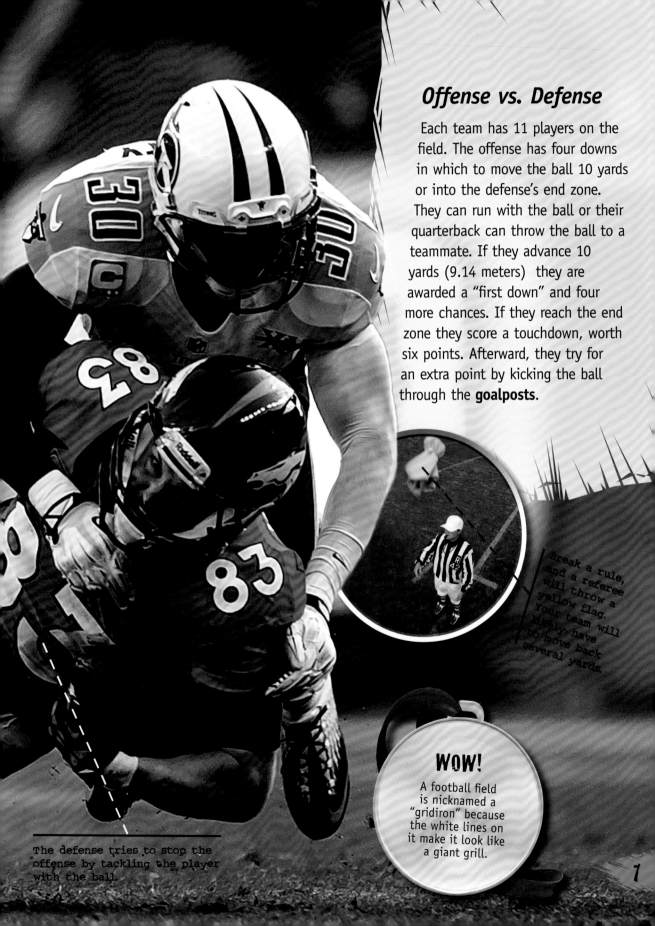

Offense vs. Defense

Each team has 11 players on the field. The offense has four downs in which to move the ball 10 yards or into the defense's end zone. They can run with the ball or their quarterback can throw the ball to a teammate. If they advance 10 yards (9.14 meters) they are awarded a "first down" and four more chances. If they reach the end zone they score a touchdown, worth six points. Afterward, they try for an extra point by kicking the ball through the **goalposts**.

Break a rule, and a referee will throw a yellow flag. Your team will likely have to move back several yards.

WOW!

A football field is nicknamed a "gridiron" because the white lines on it make it look like a giant grill.

The defense tries to stop the offense by tackling the player with the ball.

FOOTBALL EQUIPMENT

Make no mistake: football is a rough sport. Defensive players try to **tackle** the player with the ball. Offensive players can prevent this by blocking the defensive players. Several pieces of gear are used by football players of all levels.

SHOE WITH CLEATS

HIP PAD

THIGH PAD

KNEE PAD

WOW!
Workers at the Wilson Football factory in Ohio make 4,000 footballs a day and more than 700,000 a year!

Football requires a lot of gear because it's a **contact sport.** This player is about to make contact with the hard ground!

HELMET

FACE MASK

CHIN STRAP

SHOULDER PAD

JERSEY

RIB PAD

The Essentials

Players wear shoes with studs called "cleats" on the soles to grip the field. Special pads tucked inside short pants protect the hips, thighs, tailbone, and knees. A vest worn beneath the jersey shields the ribs. Shoulder pads made of plastic and foam cover the chest and shoulders. The football helmet has pads inside, filled with air or liquid, that spread the impact when a player is hit. It also has a thick face mask. Finally, don't forget the mouth guard! This simple piece of equipment helps prevent **concussions.**

More and more players today also wear gloves. These help grip the football.

The Ball

The most important piece of football equipment is the football. Its oval shape and white laces make it easier to throw and carry. Early footballs were made from inflated pig bladders. People called them "pigskins"—a nickname still used today. Today, footballs are made of cowhide or rubber. A pebbly texture is stamped onto them to make them easy to grip.

Most footballs weigh less than 1 pound (0.45 kilogram) and have two white stripes painted around them. Stripes improve the ball's visibility—especially in nighttime games.

THE QUARTERBACK

Football features a lot of positions. Eleven players are on the field for each team. Each player must do his job perfectly for the team to succeed. Let's take a look at these positions, beginning with the quarterback.

Field General

The quarterback leads the offense on the field. On each play he must quickly recognize the situation. In the **huddle**, he tells his teammates what the play will be. If the defense changes its strategy, the quarterback might shout an audible—a coded instruction to change the play. No wonder the quarterback is sometimes called the "field general!"

Some players, including quarterbacks, wear a helmet with a clear visor attached. This protects the eyes and improves visibility.

QB Greats

Many of the most popular NFL players have been quarterbacks. One of the early greats was George Blanda, who played an incredible 26 pro seasons (1949–1975). He still holds more than 10 records. Johnny Unitas also enjoyed a long career (1955–1973). He was named the NFL most valuable player (MVP) four times. Today, two of the NFL's most successful quarterbacks—and biggest stars—are Tom Brady and Peyton Manning. But soon a new crop of legends will take over.

Until the 1940s, footballers played both offense and defense. Sammy Baugh was quarterback, punter, and defensive back for the Washington Redskins from 1937 to 1952.

STAR PROFILE
TOM BRADY

Born: August 3, 1977 San Mateo, California

Team: New England Patriots

Star Stats: 6x Super Bowl champion, 3x MVP

WOW!
Drew Brees holds the record for most career passing yards: 74,437 (68,605 meters). That equals more than 42 miles (68 kilometers)!

THE RUNNING BACKS

Rushing plays are common in football. On these plays, the quarterback hands the ball to a running back. Some running backs try to use their speed to get *around* the defense. Others try to use their size to go *through* the defense.

STAR PROFILE
EMMITT SMITH

Born: May 15, 1969
Pensacola, Florida

Team: Dallas Cowboys

Star Stats: 18,355 career rushing yards, 164 career rushing touchdowns (both NFL records)

Many football fans consider Emmitt Smith to be the best running back of all time.

Fullbacks and Halfbacks

Before a play, running backs line up in the backfield behind the quarterback. There are two running back positions: fullback and halfback (sometimes called tailbacks). Fullbacks are usually bigger. They block for the halfback more than they carry the ball. Halfbacks take **handoffs**, but sometimes they catch short passes, too. For any running back, 100 rushing yards in one game is a top-notch performance.

Jim Thorpe played eight pro seasons in the 1920s. He also played pro baseball and won two Olympic gold medals in 1912!

Stars of the Backfield

Because they carry the ball so much, running backs have been some of football's biggest stars. Jim Brown played nine seasons (1957–1965) and was the NFL rushing champion for eight of them. Walter Payton was another great. His running style earned the nickname "Sweetness." Today, young stars like Ezekiel Elliott excite pro football fans with their rushing skills.

WOW!
In 2014 Samaje Perine of the University of Oklahoma set a college record by rushing for 427 yards (390 meters) in a single game!

Ezekiel Elliott of the Dallas Cowboys dodges a tackle in 2019.

13

WIDE RECEIVERS

Instead of taking handoffs, wide receivers catch passes. Passes can be as short as a few yards or 50 yards (45 meters) or more. Wide receivers make some of the most exciting plays in football.

Adam Thielen of the Minnesota Vikings hauls in a pass for a 16-yard touchdown.

WOW!
The NFL record for most touchdown catches in one game is five. Three players share the record.

STAR PROFILE
JERRY RICE

Born: October 13, 1962 Starkville, Mississippi

Teams: San Francisco 49ers, Oakland Raiders, Seattle Seahawks

Star Stats: 22,895 career receiving yards, 1,549 career receptions (both NFL records)

Going Deep

Passing plays have different routes. This is the pattern the wide receiver runs. The quarterback throws the ball so the receiver can catch it at the end of his route. This requires perfect timing. Some plays call for inside routes— the receiver runs to the middle of the field for a catch. Other plays have outside routes, where the receiver "goes deep" down a **sideline**. The receiver makes a "reception" if he catches the ball.

One-handed catches are spectacular, but players learn to catch a football with two hands.

Kings of the Catch

Wide receivers are great runners. They also are some of football's most dynamic players. Randy Moss played 14 seasons, and achieved the NFL's second most regular season touchdown catches: 156. One of today's great receivers is Larry Fitzgerald. In 2017 he caught 109 passes. But Jerry Rice is considered the greatest wide receiver ever. He once owned more than 100 NFL records!

Randy Moss's speed and pass-catching abilities earned him the nickname "Super Freak."

THE LINEMEN

Unlike other offensive linemen, the tight end is allowed to catch passes.

The largest football players are the linemen. College and NFL linemen are usually taller than 6 feet (1.8 meters). Many weigh more than 300 (136 kilograms) pounds. What do these players do that requires them to be so enormous?

STAR PROFILE
BRUCE SMITH

Born: June 18, 1963 Norfolk, Virginia

Teams: Buffalo Bills, Washington Redskins

Star Stats: 200 career sacks (NFL record), 11x Pro Bowl selection

WOW!
Aaron Gibson played in the NFL from 1999 to 2005. He stood 6 feet, 9 inches (2.06 meters) and weighed more than 400 pounds (181 kilograms).

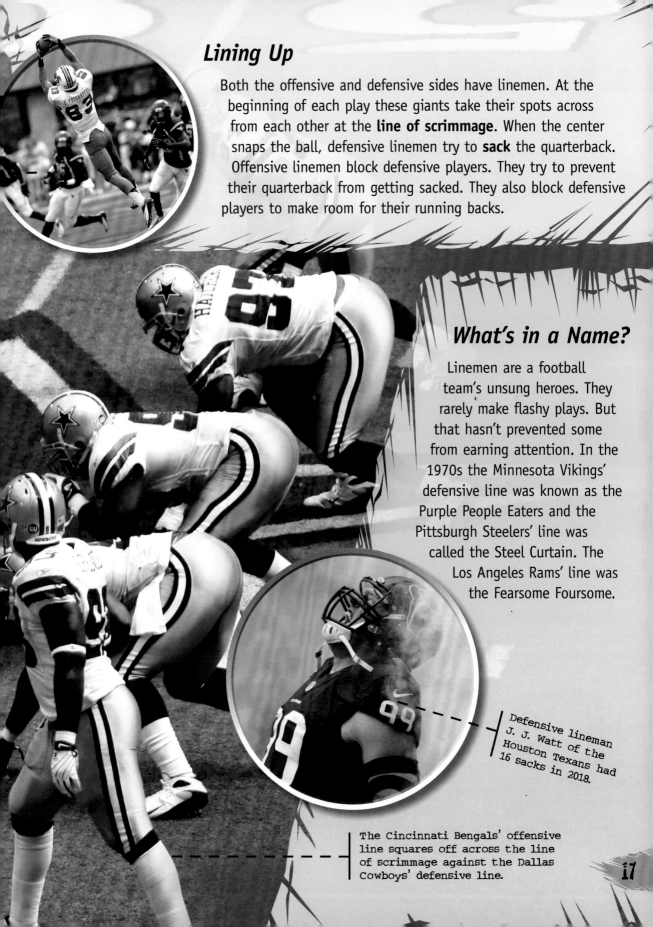

Lining Up

Both the offensive and defensive sides have linemen. At the beginning of each play these giants take their spots across from each other at the **line of scrimmage**. When the center snaps the ball, defensive linemen try to **sack** the quarterback. Offensive linemen block defensive players. They try to prevent their quarterback from getting sacked. They also block defensive players to make room for their running backs.

What's in a Name?

Linemen are a football team's unsung heroes. They rarely make flashy plays. But that hasn't prevented some from earning attention. In the 1970s the Minnesota Vikings' defensive line was known as the Purple People Eaters and the Pittsburgh Steelers' line was called the Steel Curtain. The Los Angeles Rams' line was the Fearsome Foursome.

Defensive lineman J. J. Watt of the Houston Texans had 16 sacks in 2018.

The Cincinnati Bengals' offensive line squares off across the line of scrimmage against the Dallas Cowboys' defensive line.

17

LINEBACKERS &
DEFENSIVE BACKS

Sometimes running backs break past the line of scrimmage or wide receivers streak down the field. This is when linebackers and defensive backs get in on the action.

WOW!
Linebacker Derrick Brooks played 14 seasons for the Tampa Bay Buccaneers and made 1,238 solo tackles.

One linebacker directs the defense while on the field. Clay Matthews (#52) of the Green Bay Packers is a star NFL linebacker.

Last Lines of Defense

Linebackers start the play about 5 yards (4.6 meters) behind the line of scrimmage. One linebacker directs the defense, much like the quarterback on offense. Defensive backs cover wide receivers running downfield. These "d-backs" can catch the ball, too. If they do, they get an interception and their team's offense gets the ball back.

Defensive back Jabril Peppers (#22) of Cleveland Browns is blocked by Tampa Bay Buccaneers' running back Peyton Barber (#25).

Ray Lewis was one of the most feared linebackers in the NFL. He retired in 2013.

Bruising LBs

Paul Krause set the NFL record for interceptions—he made 81 during his career with the Washington Redskins (1964–1967) and Minnesota Vikings (1968–1979). Lawrence Taylor of the New York Giants (1981–1993) was known for fearsome tackles but he could also make sacks on the **blitz** or drop back for an interception. The Baltimore Ravens' Ray Lewis was selected for 13 Pro Bowls—a linebacker record. One of today's top linebackers is Luke Kuechly. In 2018 he made 93 tackles and was named a First-team All-Pro.

PLACEKICKERS & PUNTERS

Talk about pressure! If a game is tied in the game's final seconds and his team is close to the goal line, the placekicker is called in. If he kicks a field goal through the goalposts, his team will win the game. But if he misses . . .

Golden Feet

After his team scores a touchdown, a placekicker attempts an extra point. Usually when his team reaches fourth down near the opponent's end zone, he tries for a field goal, worth three points. The punter is another **special teams** player. When his team is too far away to try for a field goal on fourth down, it's his job to **drop-kick** the ball to the opponent.

Punter Ray Guy once hit a video screen hanging from the ceiling of the Superdome with a punt.

Top Scorers

Kickers score only one or three points at a time. But over many years, those points can add up. The top 31 scorers in NFL history are placekickers! The two greatest of all time are Morten Andersen (2,544 points) and Gary Anderson (2,434 points). Both began their NFL careers in 1982, and both were experienced soccer players before playing American football.

Adam Vinatieri is the NFL's all-time leading scorer. He's played for two teams, including the Indianapolis Colts.

STAR PROFILE
MORTEN ANDERSEN

Born: August 16, 1960 Copenhagen, Denmark

Teams: New Orleans Saints, Atlanta Falcons, New York Giants, Kansas City Chiefs, Minnesota Vikings

Star Stats: 2,544 career points, 382 games played

The ball is kicked to the opposing team to begin a game or after one team has scored. For these "kickoffs," the kicker sets the ball on a rubber tee.

21

THE COACH

We've seen that a football team has a lot of players. We also learned that football is a sport of strategy and teamwork. So who directs these players and decides on a strategy? That job belongs to the head coach.

Brains behind the Brawn

A football coach can't guide a team alone. He has a large group of assistants. Some coaches help players get better at their position. Others, called coordinators, guide the offense, the defense, and special teams. Before the season the coaches create a **playbook**. This contains the plays the team will use during the season. The plays drawn on its pages use Xs and Os to represent the players.

Coaches use diagrams to teach plays to their team. Os represent the offense; Xs are the defense.

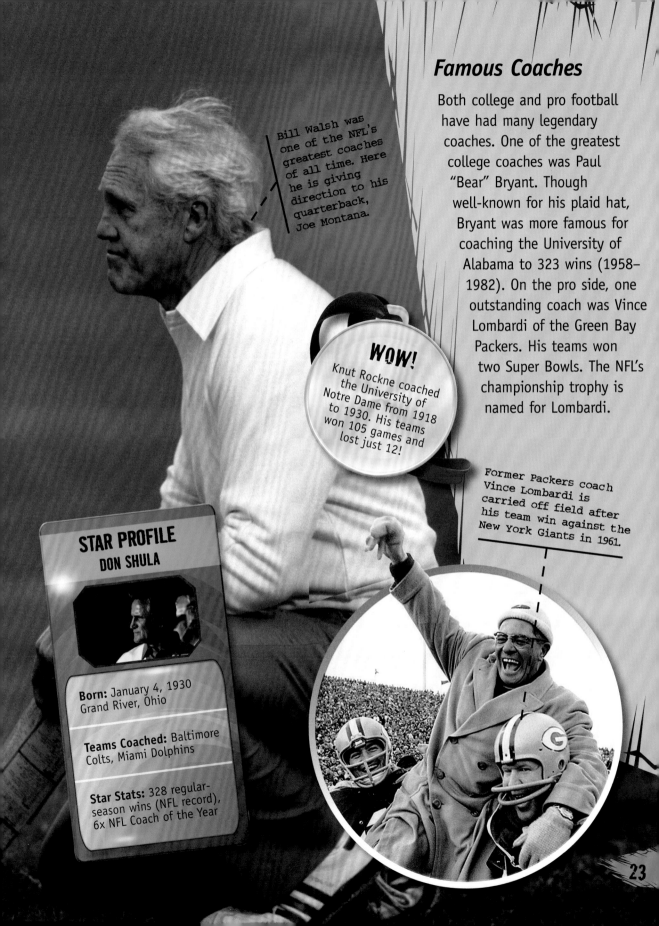

Bill Walsh was one of the NFL's greatest coaches of all time. Here he is giving direction to his quarterback, Joe Montana.

Famous Coaches

Both college and pro football have had many legendary coaches. One of the greatest college coaches was Paul "Bear" Bryant. Though well-known for his plaid hat, Bryant was more famous for coaching the University of Alabama to 323 wins (1958–1982). On the pro side, one outstanding coach was Vince Lombardi of the Green Bay Packers. His teams won two Super Bowls. The NFL's championship trophy is named for Lombardi.

WOW!

Knut Rockne coached the University of Notre Dame from 1918 to 1930. His teams won 105 games and lost just 12!

Former Packers coach Vince Lombardi is carried off field after his team win against the New York Giants in 1961.

STAR PROFILE
DON SHULA

Born: January 4, 1930 Grand River, Ohio

Teams Coached: Baltimore Colts, Miami Dolphins

Star Stats: 328 regular-season wins (NFL record), 6x NFL Coach of the Year

COLLEGE FOOTBALL

Few sports in the USA are as popular as college football. Hundreds of American colleges and universities have football teams. Every Saturday afternoon throughout the fall, these teams square off at stadiums across the country.

WOW!

Of the 20 largest stadiums in the USA, 16 are the homes of college football teams.

In the College Football Playoff National Championship 2019, the Clemson Tigers defeated the Alabama Crimson Tide 44-16.

Bowl-Bound

American football had its start at the college level. Today, the top college teams compete in the Football Bowl Subdivision (FBS). Most NFL players first play for FBS teams. FBS teams with winning records are chosen to play in bowl games at the end of the season. The winning teams from two of those bowl games go on to play for the national championship.

In the 2019 Rose Bowl Game, the Ohio State Buckeyes were matched against the Washington Huskies.

STAR PROFILE
HAROLD "RED" GRANGE

Born: June 13, 1903 Forksville, Pennsylvania
Died: January 28, 1991

Team: University of Illinois

Star Stats: 3,362 rushing yards, 31 touchdowns, 3x All-American

Heisman Heroes and Zeroes

Each year the most outstanding player in college football is awarded the Heisman Trophy. This award started in 1935. Most often, a quarterback or running back wins it. Some go on to enjoy careers in the NFL, but not all of them! Several Heisman winners, especially quarterbacks, have failed at the NFL level. Some call this the "Heisman Curse," even though many other winners have enjoyed long NFL careers.

Texas A&M quarterback Kyler Murray won the 2018 Heisman Trophy. The Heisman is made of bronze and weighs 25 pounds (11 kilograms).

25

THE PRO BOWL

Like other sports leagues, the NFL holds an all-star game each year to honor its top players. The Pro Bowl takes place the weekend before the Super Bowl. Pro Bowl players are chosen by fans, coaches, and their fellow players to take part in this special exhibition game.

From 1980 to 2016 the Pro Bowl was played at Aloha Stadium in Halawa, Hawaii.

New Rules

Football is a rough sport and the Pro Bowl is meant to be a friendly matchup. Special Pro Bowl rules lessen the chances of players getting injured. For example, there are no kickoffs after one team scores. The opponent simply takes over the ball on their own 25-yard line. In addition, defensive players are not allowed to rush kicking attempts.

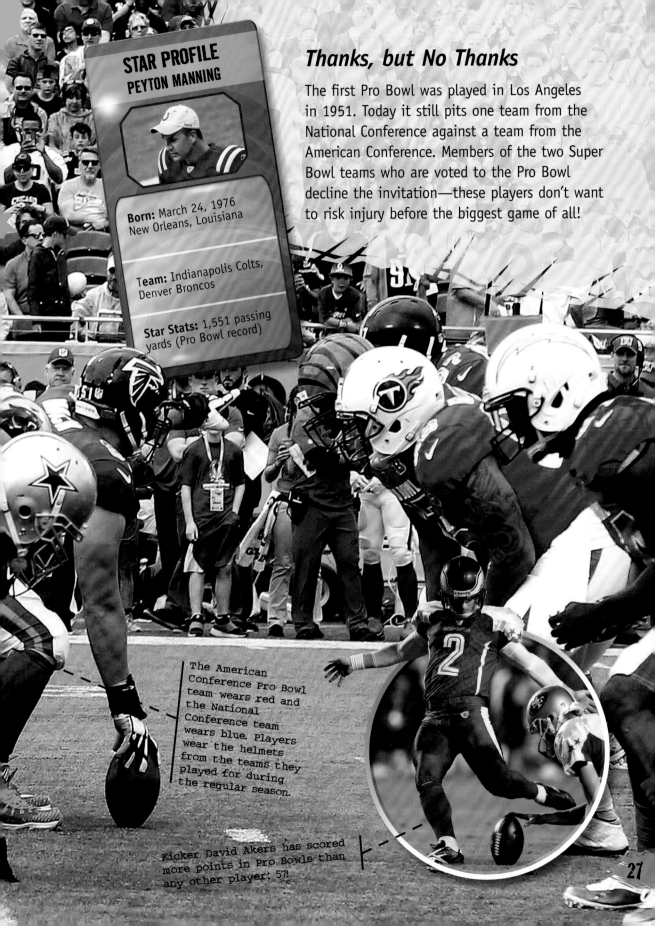

Thanks, but No Thanks

The first Pro Bowl was played in Los Angeles in 1951. Today it still pits one team from the National Conference against a team from the American Conference. Members of the two Super Bowl teams who are voted to the Pro Bowl decline the invitation—these players don't want to risk injury before the biggest game of all!

The American Conference Pro Bowl team wears red and the National Conference team wears blue. Players wear the helmets from the teams they played for during the regular season.

Kicker David Akers has scored more points in Pro Bowls than any other player: 57!

27

READY FOR SOME FOOTBALL?

College and pro football may be hugely popular in the USA, but others are enjoying time on the field, too. From grade school to high school and beyond, football fans are also playing the game.

WOW!

More than 52,000 fans gathered at AT&T Stadium in Arlington, Texas, in 2014 to watch a championship high school football game.

Turn Off the TV!

Football's a great sport for television. But many people enjoy playing, not just watching. Some families have a tradition of "touch" football games on Thanksgiving. The ball carrier is down when a defender touches them with two hands. And a lot of players start their careers with flag football. Instead of tackling, defensive players try to grab a flag from the ball carrier's belt.

In flag football, when a player has a strip of cloth, or "flag," torn from their belt, he or she is "down."

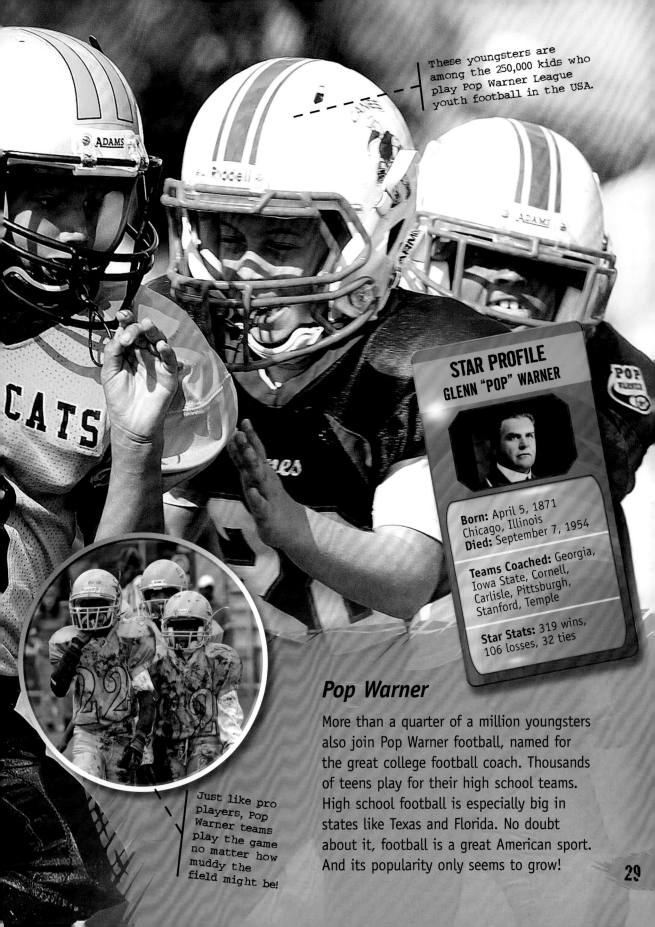

These youngsters are among the 250,000 kids who play Pop Warner League youth football in the USA.

STAR PROFILE
GLENN "POP" WARNER

Born: April 5, 1871
Chicago, Illinois
Died: September 7, 1954

Teams Coached: Georgia, Iowa State, Cornell, Carlisle, Pittsburgh, Stanford, Temple

Star Stats: 319 wins, 106 losses, 32 ties

Pop Warner

More than a quarter of a million youngsters also join Pop Warner football, named for the great college football coach. Thousands of teens play for their high school teams. High school football is especially big in states like Texas and Florida. No doubt about it, football is a great American sport. And its popularity only seems to grow!

Just like pro players, Pop Warner teams play the game no matter how muddy the field might be!

CREDITS

Key: BC = back cover, FC = front cover, t = top,
b = bottom, c = center, r = right, l = left.

Alamy: 1 OJO Images Ltd, 4-5 Chronicle, 5tl Niday Picture Library, 5bl CSU Archives/Everett Collection, 8-9 Image Source, 10-11 OJO Images Ltd, 14br Napa Valley Register/ZUMA Press, 14-15 Carlos Gonzalez/Minneapolis Star Tribune/TNS/Alamy Live News, 17bc Tribune Content Agency LLC, 21bl Aurora Photos, 26-27 Newscom/Alamy Live News, 28-29 ZUMA Press, 29bl weberfoto.

Dreamstime: 12cl Jerry Coli, 15c Brent Hathaway, 15br Scott Anderson, 16cl Jerry Coli, 19c Scott Anderson, 19bl Jerry Coli, 20br Jerry Coli, 23bl Jerry Coli, 28br Aviahuismanphotography.

Getty: FC Pete Saloutos, 2 Sean M. Haffey / Staff, 6-7 Dustin Bradford/Stringer, 12-13 Sean M. Haffey / Staff, 18-19 Robert Beck /Sports Illustrated, 19tr Icon Sportswire, 21tl Andy Lyons / Staff, 22-23 Richard Mackson, 23br Marvin E. Newman, 24-25 Jamie Schwaberow, 25tl Robert Beck, 25bl Icon Sportswire, 26br Doug Benc / Stringer, 27br Doug Benc / Stringer.

Library of Congress: 11t Harris & Ewing Collection, 13t Harris & Ewing Collection, 25cr National Photo Company Collection.

Shutterstock: BC Alex Kravtsov, 6l EKS, 7r Volt Collection, 8br Pincarel, 9cl Aspen Photo, 10br Aspen Photo, 11b Arturo Holmes, 16-17 Ken Durden, 17tl Aspen Photo, 20-21 Danny E Hooks, 22br Danny E Hooks, 27cl Alexey Stiop.

Wikimedia Commons: 12cr John Trainor, 29cr 1921 University of Pittsburgh yearbook.

AUTHOR'S NOTE

I hope you have enjoyed reading all about the history, rules, and superstars of football! Maybe you and your friends were even inspired to get outside and give football a try.

Over the years I have had the pleasure of writing books about many different topics, from hot rod cars to haunted houses, but sports have always been one of my favorite things to write (and read!) about. When I was a youngster in school, most of my reading time was spent learning about sports stars of years past. I was also lucky to participate in several sports, often at the encouragement of my parents, including ice hockey, baseball, tennis, football, golf, and even BMX racing. I was never the best among my peers in any of those sports, but it turns out that wasn't the point. I learned all about teamwork from some of my great coaches (like Lowell Thomas and Randy Reigstad), made lifelong friends, collected favorite memories, and got plenty of exercise!

Today I live in Minneapolis, Minnesota. It is known as the "City of Lakes" and it is a wonderful place to get outside and be active throughout the year. There's fishing, canoeing, bicycling, and swimming in the summer, and skating, sledding, and skiing during the long winters. The parks offer sports leagues for kids of all ages, and today I am lucky to pay forward the lessons I learned from those fantastic coaches of my youth by coaching my sons, Leo and Gus, and their ice hockey teams.

Keep reading, but keep moving, too!
Dennis Pernu

GLOSSARY

blitz
a football strategy in which linebackers and defensive backs rush the quarterback block in football, using hands and leg strength to prevent a defensive player from reaching the ball carrier

concussion
a serious head injury caused by hard contact with another player, the ground, ice, or another object

contact sport
a sport that involves contact among players or players and their equipment

drop-kick
to hold a football out in front of the body, drop it, and then kick it; also called a "punt"

goalpost
one of a pair of tall posts in each end zone through which a football is kicked to score points

handoff
the act of handing a football to a teammate; usually occurs between the quarterback and a running back

hike
the transfer of the football from the center to the quarterback to begin a play

huddle
the grouping together of a football team's offense before a play to discuss strategy

kickoff
a play in which the football is kicked from one team to the other to begin the game

line of scrimmage
the imaginary line across a football field on which a ball is set before a play

playbook
a thick book that contains diagrams of all the plays a football team uses

rushing
advancing the football up the field by carrying it

sack
the tackling of the quarterback by a defensive player behind the line of scrimmage

sideline
the line marking the edge of one long side of a football field

special teams
the offensive and defensive units that are on the field for any sort of kicking play

stats
numbers used in any sport to measure an athlete's performance

tackle
in football, using arms or hands to pull the opponent carrying the ball to the ground

31

INDEX